LOOK!

A BOOK ABOUT NATURE'S PAINTBOX

WRITTEN AND ILLUSTRATED BY JAMIE PAUL

Look at the red flower.

Flanders Poppy

Look at the red flowers.

Baja Fairy Duster

Look at the orange fish.

Japanese Koi

Look at the orange butterfly.

Monarch Butterfly

Look at the orange spines.

Chenille Prickly Pear

Look at the yellow petals.

Yellow Barrel Cactus

Look at the yellow blossom.

Arizona Poppy

Look at the yellow cactus fruits.

Barrel Cactus

Look at the green plant.

Queen Victoria Agave

Look at the green leaves.

Aspen Trees

Look at the green cactus.

Banana Yucca

Look at the bright blue sky.

Aspen Tree

Look at the light blue sky.

Silvery Lupine

Look at the lavender sky.

Silky Lupine

Look at the purple flower stalk.

Arizona Lupine

Look at the maroon cactus veins.

Dyckia Toothy

Look at the

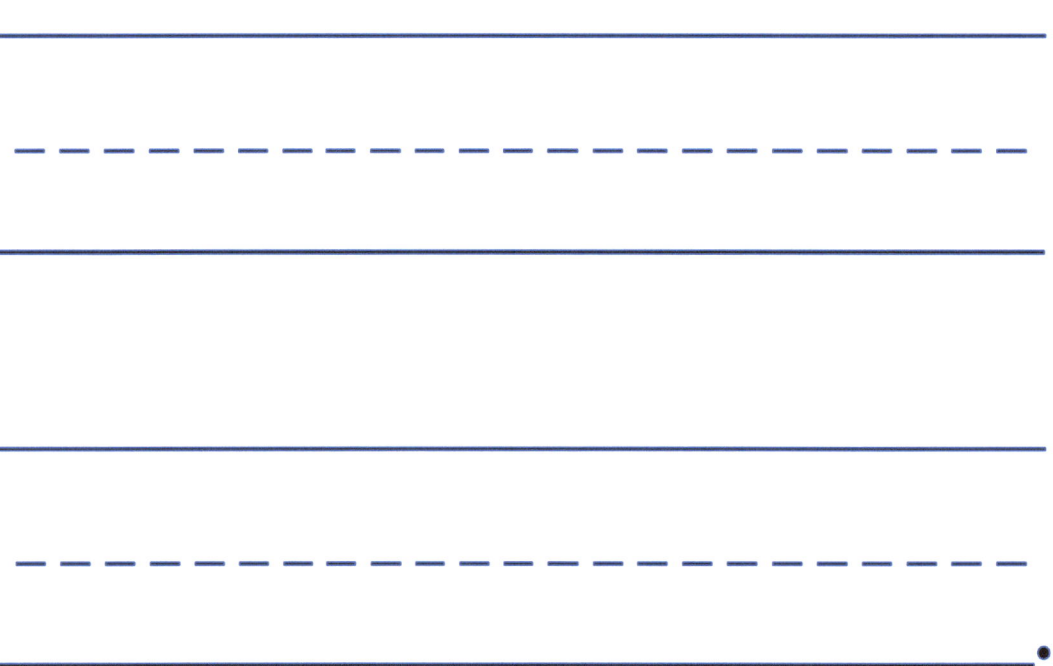

What do you see? Write the words.

What do you see? Draw the picture.